Jokes for the Rugby Club from the Blue Team

Randy Hooker

Strathearn Publishing
TRADE DISTRIBUTION
foulsham
The Publishing House, Bennetts Close,
Slough, Berks. SL1 5AP

strathearn publishing
PO Box 44, Slough, Berkshire SL1 4YN

ISBN 0-572-02046-5

Jokes contributed by Eddie Scott and many others

Printed in Great Britain by Cox & Wyman Ltd., Reading, Berkshire

YOU REALLY
SHOULDN'T TELL
STORIES LIKE THIS
YOU NAUGHTY BOY!

The German Serial

Jack Schitt was the only son of Owe Schitt the fertiliser magnate.

Jack Schitt grew up to marry Noe Alimony who, of course, became Noe Schitt.

And they had several children. Two sons, Dumb Schitt and Bull Schitt. And daughters, Lotta Schitt and Giva Schitt. Amidst their joy, however, there was sorrow too ...

(continued on page 38)

Q

What's the connection between
a dumb blonde
and a beer bottle?

A

They're both empty
from the neck up!

Auld Waalter he suck his pipe
suck ... suck ... on ... his ... pipe.

Then he say to his wife,
"Why you bother t' go iron that bra?
You got nothin' to hold up any more."

She looks him in the eye and say,
"For the same reason
I irons your pants!"

No. 8 was out of his head again ...

... and in the police station.

"I've losht my camel."

The weary duty sergeant
drags up a form and says,
"How many humps was it, sir?"

"Shcan't remember."

"Well what colour then, sir?"

"Can't remember."

***"Can you tell me anything
about your camel?"***

**"Had four legs –
and it wash ... female"**

"How do you know that, sir?"

**"'Cause on Blackfriars Bridge ...
some bugger shouted:
'Look at the cunt on that camel!'."**

A statement – fact

There's nothing inherently wrong with the word

"cunt".

A white man, stood in a gents toil[illegible]ed to glance down at the cock of the black guy [illegible] was standing [illegible]m.

"M[illegible] he ex[illegible] do you blo[illegible]s'"

"[illegible]l, said the [illegible]n. When [illegible] are young our [illegible] piece of [illegible] to our tool, and the[illegible] attach [illegible] heavy stone to the string. Eve[illegible]hat stretches our cocks."

CENSORED

**After a bitterly cold, January match ...
in the clubhouse and four pints awash,
Old Fred found himself in the privy ...**

**Well, he didn't find himself actually.
He was fumbling around with his flies
when he heard,**

***"Bit hard to find in this weather,
Fred?"***

**"Aye, tis true enuf!
Even at home ...
... when there's two
of us looking for it!"**

There was a young twerp from Bombay
Who modelled a cunt out of clay.

The heat of his prick
Turned the clay into brick

And wore all his foreskin away!

Polite Notice

for the notice board

It should be a matter of
common courtesy but

some WOMEN still fail to
lift the seat when they have finished.

In future, ladies – will you
kindly oblige.

THIS GULL DROPS A RUNNY
STREAM OF SHIT
RIGHT DOWN TRACY'S CLEAVAGE.

OUR JACK MADE THE MISTAKE
OF LAUGHING!

"Don't you bloody laugh,
Jack Hawkins –
you get a piece of paper
and wipe it clean!"

"Get a life, Trace . . .
that bird's
miles away by now!"

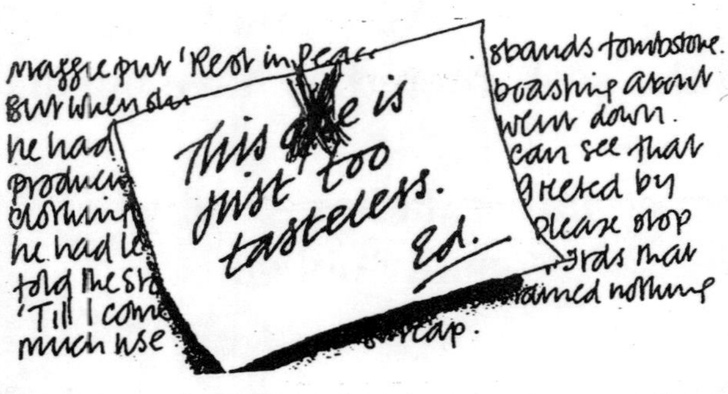

Riddle Me This

Something for the Girls

Q

I am a protrusion that comes
in many sizes.
When I am not well, I drip.
If you blow me, I feel well.
What am I?

A

A nose, my dear!

It was the wedding night and the newly-weds were laying down on the bed, getting ready to make love.

"Before we start, I think that you ought to know that one of my previous lovers was Nick Faldo."

The groom replies, "All that's in the past. As long as you love me, that's what counts."

So they proceed to do the nuptial business.

Afterwards, the groom reaches for the phone.

"Who are you calling?" asks the bride.

"Room service. Time for the champagne," he replies.

"Nick wouldn't have done that. He would have made love to me again."

So they go at it again. Afterwards, he reaches for the phone to call room service.

"Nick wouldn't have done that," she says. "He'd have made love to me again."

Tired, but keen to impress, the groom starts again.

Afterwards, the groom, exhausted, grabs the phone.

"Who are you calling?" asks the bride.

"Nick Faldo. I want to know what the par for the hole is!"

The young barmaid was [redacted] street when she [redacted] small boys [redacted] the [redacted].

"What's this [redacted]" she asked [redacted]

"It's a [redacted]" replied the boy.

"Oh," said the barmaid, "[redacted]"

"[redacted]" said the boy, "[redacted]"

**How can you spot
the waitress
amongst the other blondes?**

**She's the one
with the tampon
behind her ear,
wondering what she did
with her pencil.**

Big Mac is coming on to a wee lassie.

"Will you dance with me, hen?"
Noo, I don't like that glint in your eye.

"There's no chance
of a kiss then?"
Nooo! The glint's getting worse!

"There, I've put on
my sunglasses –
can I dance with you now?"
NOO, noo – she blushed.

"Well it can't be
the glint in me eye!"
Nooo – now it's the TILT
in your kilt!

Riddle Me This

Q

I have a stiff shaft.
My tip penetrates deep.
I come with a quiver.

A

An arrow!

The teacher was asking the children to tell her words beginning with the different letters of the alphabet.

Little Jimmy was keen to answer every time, but the teacher was reluctant to ask for his suggestions as she felt sure he would come up with a swear word.

By the time she got to R, however, she thought she had better give him a chance.

"Rhino!" cried Jimmy. "With fucking great balls!"

Last week I'm a go Los Angelos
ina big hotel.
Ina morning I go down breakfast
and I tella de waitress,
"I wanna two pisses toast."

She bringa me only one piss.
I tell her I wanna two piss.
She tella me,
"Go to the toilet then."
I explain, "You no understan,
I wanta piss on my plate."
She say you betta not piss ona dis plate.

I leave ... ana I go ... restaurant ...
Da waitress she bringa me spoon and
knife but no fock!

I tella her I wanna you give me a fock.
She tella me everyone wanna
fok from her.
I tell her she no understan,
"I wanna fock onna table."
She say you betta not fock
onna dis table.

So I go backa hotel room
and there ees no shit ona my bed.
I calls da housekeeper an I tell her,
“ I wanna shit … plis.”
She saya …me go to toilet.
I say I no unerstand
I only wanna shit onna the bed.
She tella me,
“No shit onna your bed –
   Getit!”

I decida to go – anna
   the man at the desk ee say,
“Peace to you.”
anna I say, “Piss onna you too.”

Isa funny plaice America!

Richard English – High Wycombe

Personalise this
with the name of your scrum half!

Charlie gave Sheilagh a print of the full frontal *nudie* shot he'd posed for.

He was rather *pleased* with himself!
And asked her what
she was going do with it!

"I think I'll get it ENLARGED."

Old Walt was 93;
a lovely, trusting guy,
but certainly old!

He'd remarried and she was only 33.
His doctor was explaining to him
about the expected babby!

"Let me explain it this way, Walt:

An absent-minded man went shooting
but instead of his gun, took an umbrella.
Suddenly he faced an angry bear!

Pointing the umbrella at the bear
he shot it and killed it on the spot!"

"Impossible!" cried Walt.
"Somebody else must have shot the bear."

"Exactly, Walt. That's how it happened."

Q

"What's the difference between a man and a catfish?"

A

"One's a bottom-feeding sucker the other's a fish."

20

GIRL TALK in the loo!

" Chocolate **is** better than sex ...

because when he says,
'If you love me you'll swallow this ...'
it has real meaning
when he's offering chocolate ...

**... and anyway,
chocolate is satisfying
even when it's soft!** "

We're still bugging *their* loo, lads!

"... and another reason why chocolate is better then sex – you can get it whenever you want it ... and it never has brewers' droop!"

Riddle Me This

All day long, it's in and out!
I discharge my load from my shaft!
Both men and women can go down on me!
What am I?

A

A lift!

The West Indian went to the photo counter to get his film developed.

"Do you get 36 out of your Brownie?" asked the assistant.

"I've only had 24 before, but I'd like to try!"

A word of advice about girls

The ones that crack up are the ones to get down to

"I've just done a transplant for a millionaire."

"Me too – but mine was a penis transplant."

"Well, I've just put two tits on this bloke's shoulder blades!"

"Ah but is he a millionaire?"

"No, but he will be if his arse can stand the pace!"

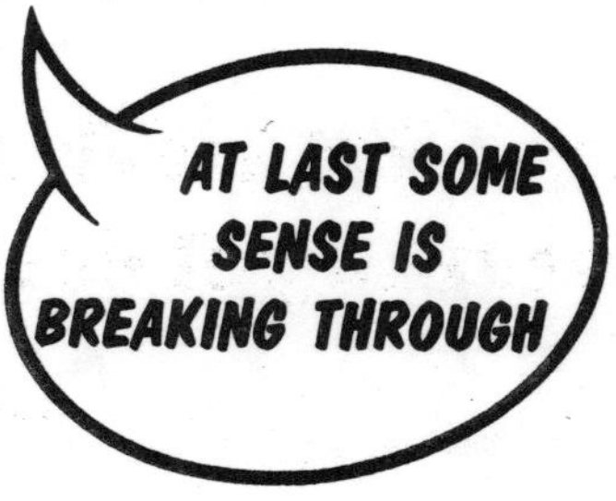

Q

If Santa Claus, a dumb blonde, a smart blonde and the tooth fairy are all walking down the street and they spot a £50 note, who picks it up?

A

The dumb blonde, stupid. There's no such thing as Santa Claus, a smart blonde or the tooth fairy!

A white man stood in a gents toilet [redacted]d to [redacted]who was standing [redacted]

“M[redacted]” he exclaimed in admiration. “How do you blokes manage to get such [redacted]es?”

DISGUSTING

“[redacted] stone to the string. Eventually that stretches our cocks.”

“[redacted] I think I'll try that!” announed the white [redacted]

A [redacted] toilet.

Riddle Me This

**My business is briefs.
I am a linguist.
I plead for it
as often as I can.
What am I?**

A

A barrister, you dick

Doctor Hung had a big reputation
in sexual problems.

If he couldn't fix you
he didn't charge –
and he was a very rich man.

Millie and Stan were his patients
and Dr Hung said he could help them.

"On your way home, I want you to buy
some grapes and a packet of doughnuts
to play with.

"Millie, you will sit on the floor with your
legs open and from across the room Stan
will flick his grapes
until he makes a *bull's eye*
in your love canal.

Stan will then *slowly* retrieve his
grape using only his tongue.

And you, Stan, will also sit so that Millie
can toss her doughnuts
at your love pole
until one makes a ringer on your tool.

Millie will then crawl slowly towards it and *consume* it – every mouthful."

Well do you know, it worked!
Their sex life was transformed.

So their friends Ted and Alice saw Dr Hung
and he reached an amazing conclusion …
"I can't help! You've got as good as it gets."

Alice was *distraught.*
Her eyes filled with tears …
and Dr Hung was so touched that he said,
"Well, we can but try then …

On your way home I want you to buy
some things to play with.

I want you, Ted, to go into the fruit shop
and buy a big bunch of grapes.

And you Alice …
must go to the tobacconist
and buy a packet of
Polos …"

Did you hear about Trevor?
It was a laugh!

He got caught on the job ...
And bollock naked he had to escape down the drainpipe.

Lucky bastard reached the bottom in the middle of a marathon!
So he joined it to make a perfect escape.

But one of the runners said to him,

"You doing it that way for charity?"

"Yes," says Trev, "for a ... *naturist beach.*"

"And do you always wear a condom?"

"Only when it's raining."

Stunning!
'til she opened her mouth!

**"Hi there beautiful.
What's your star sign?"**

Herpes, ya twerp!

**Snow White
woke up feeling happy.
But only 'til
Happy got out of bed!**

James Spink – London

No 8 met this darling little blonde
and just fell in love – ya know,
like he does!

He knew he couldn't *chat her up* ...
so he went to Smoothie Bob for a lesson.

"Just be yourself and say something easy
to get the conversation going."

"Like what?" said No 8.

"Well something like 'nice day isn't it?'"

"... and then what?"

"Well you can try saying ...
'*And it was nice yesterday too!*' or maybe,
'*They say it's going to be good tomorrow*',
anything that comes into your head
to keep the conversation going ...
anything – just be yourself!"

Well next time No 8 saw her,
she was exiting the public loo.
And bravely he opened up:

"Hello! Lovely day isn't it?"

"Yes it is – marvellous."

She gave him a warm smile and he was encouraged.

> "Yesterday was great too,
> didn't you think?"

"It certainly was," and she beamed again. No 8 was in and working his socks off!

> "... and tomorrow too they say."

Then his mouth went dry ...
he was looking into the most beautiful pair of blue eyes and all he could remember was ... be yourself ... be yourself.

And he blurted out:

> "... Just been for a shit then?"

R Hollingworth – Kent

RASTAS, YOU'S A PAIN! YOU GETS RIGHT UP MY NOSE!
LISA, YOU KNOW RIGHT WELL THAT'S THE ONLY PLACE I HASNT PUT IT... YET!

32

Mrs Murphy be shouting at Mrs McGinty across the road – in fighting mood!

"Hey missus!
Why has yo been sayin'
that moy old man
has a wart on the end of his cock!"

" Sure oi said no such thing ...
I *never* said he had a wart
on the end of his cock.

"Oi just said ...
it felt like one!"

P. Smith – Gillingham

We're in Africa on Safari.
And our Horny Hero is about to drop a bloody great elephant
with his big barrel gun.

Just as he is about to pull the trigger,
a little head appears at the end of his sight
and this goblin's voice says:

" 'ere you can't shoot a wonderful animal like that!
You go off home now – and if you do
I will grant you one wish.
What do you want it to be?"

Our Horny Hero doesn't have to give it much thought.

"OK it's a deal –
and for my wish I want one as big as that elephant."

"Done! And when you get home
your wish will be granted."

Homewards travelled Horny –
flicking through his little black book
to see which of his lovely lady friends
was to share his new endowment.

He entered the house
full of great expectations and …
he sort of sagged in half …

He'd made a complete cunt of himself.

F. H.WESTNIP – Chatham

The fullback was in the bar bitching and boring again.

"So far this season ...
... I've still only struck
three bloody balls properly."

... and this voice mutters
out of its beer pot ...

"... for two of those you
had to step on that rake
in the garden!"

A white man stood in a gents toilet [redacted] d to [redacted] who was standing [redacted].

"M[redacted] he exclaimed in admiration. "How do you blokes manage to get such [redacted]es?"

DISGUSTING

"[redacted]" s[redacted] the [redacted]ck[redacted]ma[redacted]. Whe[redacted] w[redacted] a[redacted] ou[redacted] m[redacted] ers [redacted] str[redacted] tool, and the[redacted] a[redacted] stone to the string. Eventua[redacted]y that stretches our cocks."

"[redacted] I think I'll try that!" announed the white [redacted]

A [redacted] ag[redacted] toilet.

THE HONEYMOON NIGHT IT WAS

**OUR JACK IS CLIMBING THE STAIRS
TO HIS PRETTY LITTLE VIRGIN WIFE.
HE ENTERS THE ROOM TO FIND HER
WITH NOTHING ON EXCEPT THE RADIO.**

AND AS WHITE AS A SHEET.

**"Oh Jack … JACK …
we've had a burglar"**

"Did he take anything?"

**"YES Jack he did …
I thought he was you!!"**

Advertising Slogans
that definitely didn't travel —

From its manufacturers in Sweden …

Nothing Sucks Like Electrolux

The Hard Schitt Saga ...

(continued from page 4)

Unfortunately the great shoveller in the sky took their middle daughter when she was but a baby.
She had been christened Holy Schitt.
But apart from this dark chapter in their lives, it has to be said that they were as happy as pigs in ...

(continued on page 44)

System Bug Warning

Wife 1.0 has an undocumented bug. Do NOT try to install software program Mistress 1.0 before de-installing Wife 1.0.

Wife 1.0 can delete MSMoney files before executing a self-uninstallation. Mistress 1.0 will in most cases refuse to install with the error message: *'Insufficient system resources'.*

System Bug Warning

Girlfriend 2.0

Never install Girlfriend 2.0 on top of Girlfriend 1.0.

There is an inexplicable conflict over the shared use of the I/O port.

Three men were talking in a bar one evening ...

The Englishman stated proudly that he had 10 CHILDREN ... One more and he could have had a FOOTBALL TEAM ...

The Welshman said he could beat that as he had 12 CHILDREN and he would only need three more for a RUGBY TEAM ...

The Arab said proudly that he could beat them all, as he had 18 WIVES, which as he pointed out ...

... was enough holes for a GOLF COURSE.

Q

I'm spread before I'm eaten.
Your tongue gets me off.
People sometimes lick my nuts.
What am I?

A

Peanut butter.

Where's the best place to fuck the sheep, Joe?

Oi does it right on the edge of that precipice.

'cause then I finds that they pushes back harder!

Mike Williams – Devon

Roger was 52 – and vain …

He was on youth pills, fake tan and HRT!

The sort of bloke that asks how old you think he is.
Which he did – to the butcher as it happens.
And he thought Roger was 32! Roger loved it.

Later in the bus shelter he was alone with a charming little old lady – and he couldn't resist asking:

"How old do you think I am?"

"Oh I don't know dear – I'm no good on faces. But I know I could tell if I saw your member."

So utterly charming was she … that our Roger got it out!

And she had a right good fondle and feel for five minutes – which Roger rather enjoyed, it has to be said.

"You're 52."

"How do you know that?" cried Roger.

And she blushed as she said, "I'm afraid, my dear,
I was behind you at the butchers!"

This club was on its annual tour.
They had an address to billet six of the lads and everyone was off the bus except Cox who was sleeping it off!

They knocked on the door and it was opened by this very sexy, rather tarty, blond bit of rough. And the coach said,

"I'm told that you are going to put up some of the lads miss."

"Well I certainly hope so! How many do I get – there's room for plenty!"

"Well I've got five left without Cox."

And she slammed the door in his face!

Q

What do you call the gay props in the Scottish front row?

A

Ben Dover and Phil McCrack.

The Hard Schitt Saga

(continued from page 38)

Time passed and the family prospered. Deep Schitt married a pretty little drop-out called Dumb Bow to become Dumb Schitt and Bull married a spicy little Italian number *Pisa* ...

(To be continued in our next book!)

Q

What's the similarity between Brussels sprouts and pubic hair?

A

You push them both to one side and carry on eating.

A newly married couple, Tim and Georgina, retire to their honeymoon bedroom at the hotel.

As they undress in front of each other for the first time, Tim says, 'Darling, what a lovely big arse you've got.'

With this, Georgina slaps him round the face and pushes him out on to the balcony, dressed only in his socks.

He's out there in the cold, freezing his nuts off, when the man in the next room is also pushed out on to the balcony.

'Shit,' he says, 'it's my wedding night and I've been thrown out for saying my wife had big tits.'

A third man appears on the next balcony. 'I bet you've really put your foot in it,' says Tim.

'No,' says the man. 'But I bloody well could have!'

Paul Brewer – Dorset

Q

What's the difference between butter and a dumb blonde?

A

Butter is difficult to spread!

Alec, Bob and Colin are discussing what they are going to get their wives for Christmas.

'This year,' says Alec, 'I'm getting my wife a necklace and a silk scarf. That way, if she doesn't like the necklace, she can cover it up with the scarf.'

Bob says, 'I'm doing something similar. I'm getting her a ring and a pair of gloves. If she doesn't like the ring, she can cover it up with the gloves.'

'Well,' says Colin, 'I'm getting my wife a hat and a dildo and if she doesn't like the hat she can go and fuck herself!'

Snow White is standing outside the dwarves' cottage looking radiantly happy.

"And I always thought 7-Up was a drink!"

A dashing young scrum half called Dave
Kept a dead whore in a cave.

He must have had pluck,
To have a cold fuck …

… but think of the money he'd save!

An Irish golfer goes to his priest and says, "Father – I have a confession to make – I used the F-word."

The priest says, "Tell me about it, son."

"Well, I'd tee'd off and the ball went straight into the woods."

"Is that when you used the F-word?" says the priest.

"No, I did an excellent recovery shot, but then I sliced the ball into a bunker!"

"Then you used the F-word?" the priest enquired.

"No. Again I played a superb shot and it landed within six inches of the hole."

There was a pause ... then the priest said, "Don't tell me you missed the fucking putt!"

Graham – Gloucestershire

Mickey Mouse is in his lawyer's office.

"Well, Mickey," says the lawyer. "I can see you want to divorce Minnie, but you'll need better grounds than saying her teeth stick out."

"I didn't say her teeth stick out – I said she was fucking Goofy!"

Q

What's better than daffodils on your piano?

A

Two lips on your organ!

A winger from Chorlton-cum-Havery,
Had habits most unsavoury.

With maniacal howls,
He buggered young owls.

Which he kept in an underground aviary.

There was a young full back from Cosham.
Who took out his bollocks to wash 'em.

His wife said, "Jack,
If you don't put them back.

I'll tread on the fuckers and squash 'em!"

Bob has had a really hard Saturday.

A few pints at lunch time, then a really hard game, followed by a monstrous piss-up in the bar afterwards.

He suddenly realises that he is two hours late for a date with his girlfriend.

"Don't worry," says the club coach. "Take her a big bunch of flowers. It always works."

So, off Bob goes to his girlfriend's flat, stopping on the way for a large bouquet of flowers.

He arrives at the flat and rings the bell.

Sure enough, the flowers work. His late arrival is forgotten and his girlfriend disappears enthusing about the flowers.

After a few minutes, Bob wonders where she has gone and goes to look for her.

He finds her in the bedroom, lying on the bed stark naked, with her legs wide apart.

"Darling, this is for the flowers," she says.

"What?" says Bob. "Haven't you got a vase?"

Little Johnnie is playing at school, when he cuts his finger on a pair of scissors.

He runs to the teacher. "Mrs Brown, I've cut my finger. Have you got any cider?"

The teacher is puzzled. "What do you want cider for, Johnnie?" she asks.

"Well miss, I heard my sister saying that when she gets a prick in her hand she always puts it in cider!"

Overheard the next day

"How did it go last night?
... Did she like it?"

Yeah – but she prefers it in her ear.

"What makes you think that!"

***When I tried to stick it
in her mouth
she kept turning her head.***

Q

**When do we let the blondes
take a coffee break?**

A

**We never let them have
a coffee break –
it takes too long to retrain them.**

A man walks into the pub and goes up to the bar.

He hears this voice saying, 'Good day sir, and what a super suit you have on, it fits you so well and must have cost you a fortune.'

The man looks around him and can't see anyone at all. All of a sudden he hears the voice again, 'My goodness sir, your haircut is so perfect. I wish all our customers could look as fine as you.'

The man looks all around him but there is no one near him at all. Really confused now, he looks behind the bar, under his feet, looks for microphones, etc.

Again, he hears the same voice. 'Sir, I bet you have all the luck with the ladies with your prosperous looks and obvious charm.'

The barman appears and asks if he can help the man. The man says, 'Well, I keep hearing this voice speaking to me but I can't see anyone around.'

The barman says, 'Oh, don't worry sir, that's just the peanuts, they're complimentary.'

Snow White, one of the dwarves and Quasimodo are having a drink one day.

"Do you know," said Snow White. "I am definitely the most beautiful person in the whole world."

"Of course you are," said the dwarf, "and I am definitely the smallest person in the world."

"Yeah," said Quasimodo. "And there is no doubt that I am the ugliest person on the planet."

"Tell you what,' said Snow White, "let's go down to the Guinness Book of Records and register our claims."

They arrive at the offices of the Guinness Book of Records and go in one at a time to register their various claims to fame.

Snow White comes out and says to the other two, "Told you so – I am the most beautiful person in the world. They're putting me in the next edition of the book."

A few minutes later the dwarf comes out. "There you go, the smallest person in the world – no problem."

Quasimodo goes into the office and there follows a heated argument which can be heard outside.

Finally, he comes out, turns to the others, and asks:

"Just who the fuck is Ginger Spice?"

A white man stood in a gents toilet [redacted] d to [redacted] who was standing [redacted]

"M[redacted] he exclaimed in admiration. "How do you blokes manage to get [redacted] es?"

DISGUSTING

"[illegible]," s[illegible] the [illegible]ck ma[illegible]. Whe[illegible] w[illegible] a[illegible] ou[illegible] m[illegible] ers [illegible] a p[illegible] o[illegible] stri[illegible] o [illegible] tool, and the[illegible] e[illegible] a[illegible] h a [illegible] ea[illegible] y stone to the string. Eventually that stretches our cocks."

[redacted] I think I'll try that!" announed the white [redacted]

A [redacted] ag[redacted] toilet.

OFF TO THE RACES

Time:	**Midnight**
Distance:	**All the way**
Purse:	**£200.00**
Weather:	**Very Drunk**
Track:	**Drippy**

Odds	**Name**
2–1	Bare Belly
5–1	Passionate Lady
100–1	Conscience
6–1	Heavy Bosom
3–1	Cherry
2–1	Silk Panties
100–1	Clean Sheets
3–1	Big Dick
5–1	Thighs
5–1	Jockey Shorts
Evens	Douche Bag

THEY'RE OFF

Conscience is left at the post. Silk Panties and Jockey Shorts are off with a rush. Bare Belly is beginning to show. Heavy Bosom with Clean Sheets at the back. Douche Bag is completely lost.

AT THE RAIL

It's Bare Belly on top. Thighs open up a hole and Big Dick is going in. Heavy Bosom is hard pressed. Passionate Lady is coming strong and Conscience is completely lost.

AT THE TURN

It's Cherry between Big Dick and Passionate Lady. Thighs working hard and Bare Belly is under terrific pressure.

AT THE STRETCH

Cherry cracks under the strain as Big Dick goes in for the kill. Passionate Lady is doing her best and Bare Belly is close up. Big Dick passed Thighs by a full length and Passionate Lady is almost overcome.

AT THE FINISH

Big Dick rushes in, but Passionate Lady takes all he has and it's a dead heat. Heavy Bosom folds, Bare Belly is all lathered up at the finish. Thighs pull up and Clean Sheets never had a chance, while Conscience wasn't even in the race from the start. Big Dick unexpectedly gives a quick spurt and Passionate Lady kept coming. Douche Bag came in last to clean up the track.

Harry was turned on by a blue video at his mate's house and thought he had hit upon the secret of livening up his sex life.

When he arrived home, he said to his wife,

"When we make love tonight, I want you to moan and groan when I tell you."

His wife agreed, so when they were beginning to get it together, Harry said,

"Okay, start moaning!" and his wife said,

"So when are you going to wallpaper this room. And do you have to go down the pub again tonight ..."

The young barmaid was [redacted] street
when she [redacted] small boys
[redacted] the [redacted].
"What's this [redacted]?" she asked [redacted]
"It's a [redacted]" replied the boy.
"Oh," said the barmaid, "[redacted]"
"[redacted]" said the boy, "[redacted]"

Q

How far could you see if you had a nine-inch penis on your head?

A

You couldn't see at all – you'd have a pair of bollocks covering your eyes!

We're not getting enough!

And we're certainly not getting it regularly! C'mon guys we need more jokes and one liners. If you don't perform, there won't be another collection – 'cos I've run out of good ones!

If you hear a funny story and think that it would be good for our next collection, then just send it in.

If we publish *your* joke in the next book, we will acknowledge you as its author and send you a free copy containing your name in print.

You can then flash the book round the pub to show how famous you have become. And insist that those who wish to remain in your company buy you drinks in recognition of your achievement!

Yours for a laugh.

ED.
Strathearn Publishing

P.S. You'll find our address on the back of the title page. Where we have more than one submission of the same joke, then it will be the first received which will be given the credit.